Wild Plants in Flower

Moccasin Flower

Wild Plants in Flower— Wetlands and Quiet Waters of the Midwest

Photographs and Introduction by
Torkel Korling

Essay and Species Notes by
Robert O. Petty and Anne M. Petty

With a Foreword by
Marion T. Jackson

AN IMPRINT OF
INDIANA UNIVERSITY PRESS
BLOOMINGTON AND INDIANAPOLIS

A PUBLICATION OF
Quarry Books
AN IMPRINT OF

Indiana University Press
601 North Morton Street
Bloomington, Indiana 47404-3797 USA

http://iupress.indiana.edu

Telephone orders	800-842-6796
Fax orders	812-855-7931
Orders by e-mail	iuporder@indiana.edu

Essays and species notes © 2005 by Anne M. Petty
Photographs © 2005 by Diane Korling

All rights reserved

No part of this book may be reproduced or utilized in any form or by any means, electronic or mechanical, including photocopying and recording, or by any information storage and retrieval system, without permission in writing from the publisher. The Association of American University Presses' Resolution on Permissions constitutes the only exception to this prohibition.

The paper used in this publication meets the minimum requirements of American National Standard for Information Sciences—Permanence of Paper for Printed Library Materials, ANSI Z39.481984.

Manufactured in China

Library of Congress Cataloging-in-Publication Data

Korling, Torkel.
  Wetlands and quiet waters of the Midwest / photographs and introduction by Torkel Korling ; essay and species notes by Robert O. Petty and Anne M. Petty ; with a foreword by Marion T. Jackson.
    p. cm. — (Wild plants in flower ; [4])
  Includes bibliographical references and index.
  ISBN 0-253-21766-0 (pbk. : alk. paper)
  1. Wetland plants—Middle West. 2. Wild flowers—Middle West. 3. Wetland ecology—Middle West. I. Petty, Anne M. II. Title.
  QK128.K67 2005
  581.7'68'09772—dc22
                                    2004025488

1 2 3 4 5 10 09 08 07 06 05

TITLE PAGE FRONTIS

Moccasin Flower
Cypripedium acaule / ORCIDACEAE

Seen here by evening light in late May, a wild orchid shares its habitat with Marsh Cinquefoil (*also see* p. 29) beside a shallow lake in Michigan. Often heralding the edge of a lake, marsh, or wet bog, the plant may, however, thrive in dry sandy pine or oak woods as well. The limiting factor here is not water but an acid substrate required by essential symbiotic fungi (on the orchid's roots) that assist in nutrient uptake. Indians made a soothing "tea" from powdered root, giving us the common name Nerve-Root; the name Moccasin Flower is said to honor a heroic Ojibwa woman. Basal leaves attach directly to the stem (*acaule*), for which the plant is sometimes called the Stemless Lady's-slipper. Becoming rare to infrequent in the wild due to loss of habitat and transplanting, this plant's endangered status serves as metaphor for our dwindling wetlands.

When this book was first written (originally planned as part of a five-volume set entitled *Wild Plants in Flower*), wetlands were already an endangered habitat with numerous species of plants and animals at risk. Now, more than twenty-five years later, their preservation is still of great concern. And the need to enlist support for saving our remaining wetlands continues to be urgent.

This volume is dedicated to the memory of Robert O. Petty (1933–1990) and Torkel Korling (1903–1998). Both spent much of their lives observing and recording natural landscapes and the wondrous species they support. Mr. Korling told his story with luminous photographs; Dr. Petty wove his message with words, scientific as well as poetic. The images and writing within this volume preserve a record of a vanishing native flora. It is hoped this book will inspire a new generation of environmentally aware citizens to commit themselves to saving the wild areas described herein as well as other natural landscapes.

ANNE M. PETTY
2004

CONTENTS

FOREWORD BY MARION T. JACKSON   ix
PREFACE BY ROBERT O. PETTY   xiii
INTRODUCTION BY TORKEL KORLING   xv

>Prologue / 1
>Remembrance / 4
>Making Land / 12
>Habitat / 20
>Adaptations / 30
>Succession / 50
>Resilience / 62
>Epilogue / 82

SUGGESTIONS FOR FURTHER READING   91
TORKEL KORLING'S WILDFLOWER PHOTOGRAPHY   95
INDEX TO PLANTS PICTURED   97

Foreword

For uncounted millennia humans have been drawn to wetlands and quiet waters for their habitations. The presence of abundant food along the shorelines and in the waters themselves, a plentiful supply of fresh water, plus associated fertile soils for growing crops, collectively made the life of early peoples much easier at localities adjacent to stream courses and wetlands. Besides, waterways were the easiest travel routes through wilderness areas. Our human sojourn has largely been a quest for benevolent, well-watered landscapes.

To witness the profusion of both plant and animal life that a dry landscape can potentially support, only water needs to be added, be it farm pond, a re-flooded marsh, or a restored wetland. Create aquatic habitat and they will come—cattail and marsh marigold, bulrush and buttonbush, bladderwort and showy ladyslipper, dragonflies and whirligig beetles, frogs and salamanders, muskrat and mink, waterfowl, herons, and shorebirds—all intermingled among countless grasses, sedges, and beautiful wetland wildflower species.

Most students of nature are less knowledgeable about wetland plants than those of forests and prairies. And perhaps with good reason. Unfortunately, our fascination with wild wetlands and quiet waters is tempered with a worry that aquatic habitats may harbor swarms of mosquitoes or other irksome insects, or perhaps poisonous reptiles or plants. Such fears are largely unfounded, and may detract from our enjoyment of the great biodiversity present in areas possessing abundant standing water, but such is the nature of human bias.

Many Midwestern wetlands are a gift of the glaciers, as the receding ice left natural lakes and depressions almost without number across lands north of the southern glacial terminus. Meltwater and abundant rainfall near the ice margin quickly filled low-lying landscapes. Waves of wildflowers accompanied their forest associates as the vegetation migrated geographically across the deglaciated landscapes, as climates warmed during the millennia of the Pleistocene summer that we continue to enjoy. Other sequences of plant species followed in decades-long successional advances as habitats at a given location were colonized and the vegetation matured. In addition, each year's seasonal advance results in another kaleidoscope of flowering patterns that differ weekly throughout the growth season. Consequently, it is necessary to visit wetland areas frequently for full enjoyment of the wildflowers present. The only constant in nature is change.

A French proverb states that "Man strides across the land and deserts follow in his footsteps." In the wake of settlement a drier landscape has resulted. The American Midwest is no exception. For example, an estimated 5.6 million of Indiana's 23 million acres were originally wetlands—upland swamp forest, floodplains, wet prairies, marshes, fens, and bogs. Now less than 15 percent of that original wetland acreage remains. The surrounding states of Ohio, Michigan, and Illinois have witnessed similar declines in wetland habitat. Forest clearing, drainage, ditching, filling, stream alteration, and lakeshore development have all taken their toll. Populations of aquatic plant and animal species have declined drastically in concert since presettlement days, as wetland acreage has shrunk.

A summary example is the fabled Kankakee Marsh of northwestern Indiana. During the early decades of the twentieth century, productive wetlands there harbored waterfowl and shorebird numbers that darkened the sun when taking flight. Likewise, those marshes and wet prairies were filled with an unrivaled pageant of wildflowers that almost defied description. Now, a mere fragment of the Kankakee remains intact.

But help is on the way to retain the wetlands that remain, and, at numerous locations, wetland restoration is actively in progress. Most of the best marshes, fens, and bogs of the upper Midwest are now protected as dedicated state nature preserves. The Nature Conservancy has active acquisition and restoration projects at both Kankakee Marsh (and associated dry uplands) and the Limberlost Swamp (of Gene Stratton-Porter fame) in northeastern Indiana. As these and many other wetland areas are protected and restored ecologically, aquatic plant and animal species will quickly recolonize the renewed habitats.

This book is a beautiful tribute to wetland natural areas and their component wildflower species. The late Dr. Robert O. Petty was an astute ecologist, brilliant essayist and poet, untiring spokesman for nature preservation, and my closest professional friend. It is indeed an honor and a rare privilege to write an introduction to one of his last, and quite possibly his finest, piece of nature writing. The story that unfolds in this little volume—in exquisite photographs by the late Torkel Korling, perceptive essays, and revealing wildflower species descriptions—is a most moving experience in nature appreciation. Savor every image and word. If only *I* could practice the craft of nature interpretation as well as did Torkel Korling and Robert O. Petty. . . .

For Bob—with Great Affection and Admiration,

> MARION T. JACKSON
> Professor Emeritus of Ecology
> Indiana State University
> July 10, 2004

Preface

Lake country and wetlands! These are habitats that comprise less than 6 percent of our continent, even when adding all the coastal wetlands, and they are disappearing fast. They are worth a closer look. This volume provides a brief look at freshwater wetlands and quiet waters, something of their past and present, something of their rich ecological and genetic legacy—their special gift of life to the land around them. What follows are some of the representative species of this habitat as photographed by one of the most ecologically perceptive artists I have known.

Robert O. Petty
1978

Introduction

With this fourth volume in the *Wild Plants in Flower* series we revisit some of the ground covered in our prairie, boreal forest, and deciduous forest books, and wade into the wet places, seasonally or permanently flooded or with a high-water table, to focus on an assemblage of flowering plants uniquely defined by their ability to survive and prosper in saturated soils.

Dr. Robert O. Petty, late professor of biology at Wabash College, Crawfordsville, Indiana, provides narrative detail both learned and eloquent on the habitats of these species, their ecology, and natural history. In addition to many technical papers, Dr. Petty published poems, essays, and articles in a variety of books and journals, including most recently *Eastern Deciduous Forest* in this series, and in the National Geographic Society's books *Wilderness USA* and *Our Continent*.

The plants shown in flower here can give only a hint of the rich diversity nurtured in the many types of North American wetlands; for explication of the sedges and rushes and their grassy kin, you must look elsewhere. Of the species illustrated, the majority have broad and, in some cases, circumboreal ranges, but a summer visitor to wet ground in the Midwest region of the Great Lakes should find many familiar, and here may make new, acquaintances in several plant families. Classic botanical illustration has been my model as I have tried to include identifying detail particular to a species, while suggesting in the photographic setting each plant's physical habitat, pattern of growth, and common associates, the ecological context. It is toward the continued recognition and preservation of natural environments that this book is dedicated.

TORKEL KORLING
1978

Wild Plants in Flower

Prologue

It is a morning of that summer when I want to explore the lake country—a refuge more real than legend, more than a memory of dream-fragments, the remnants of a vanished time. I drive through river towns, across long iron bridges, over the oxbow sloughs and old meanders, past cypress and tupelo swamp, along miles of willow and cottonwood, soft maple and elm.

I continue north across the branches of the Mississippi drainage, up from Reelfoot Lake to the lower river valley of the Ohio and the Wabash, the White River and the Tippecanoe. Wetlands! I stop to rest. Nearby a tall dark trestle spans a shallow lake. Damp evening air is now its only freight, filling twilight niches of cat-tails and lily pads, spatterdock and water-arum. Soon, along this timeless floodplain corridor, the once-vast flock of waterfowl will be edging south; ducks and geese circling, feeding, following the remnant wetlands.

But where is that northern source, where maples flag red and sunlight flashes in the stuttering yellow leaves of birch and aspen? I can remember the pungency, the green of pine and spruce around the lakes. I want to see once more the lakes of childhood memory—wild, unspoiled. But how far north must I go? I do not get there. Time is running out.

The once wild lakes at an easy distance are peopled now, ringed with summer places. Elegant year-round homes stretch their lawns down to boat docks and cleared swimming beaches. Marginal "waterweeds" have been cleaned away. Here and there a thin scatter of bulrush rides out the prop wash and grazing water skis. In a few places the shoreline vegetation burgeons, wondrous and diverse—cat-tail and spatterdock, pond-lily, water-plantain. Shoreward they nod—swamp milkweed, angelica, and boneset. At the wet wood's edge, a sudden cardinal-flower or tall swamp-candle stands, in mottled sunlight, as do nearby thickets of buttonbush. Everywhere I see the old tenacity—audacious life staking transient claim on space and time, its light-woven colors framed in silence and shadow. And memory. But time is running out.

Remembrance

We remember a place in time—in human consciousness. We were there. A hundred centuries ago we came upon that vast drowned land. It seemed we walked into a foreverness of lakes and marshes, the brief nights spinning into dawn. Children of the glacier, we hunted the great herds; then, with the fierce winter, tracked them south. Far to the north and east lay the blue-gray paternal ice, still a half-mile thick. At summer's end and throughout the dwindling light of autumn, a great wind-howl roared from the frozen waste. It swept over gravel tundra, across the withered sedge and stunted trees. Those sounds of wind and the wet gray skies still haunt us with old meanings.

Floating-leaved Pondweed
Potamogeton natans / NAJADACEAE

No plant family on earth occupies a more critical place in the current of life or the flow of energy in freshwater lakes than do the pondweeds. More than sixty perennial species of *Potamogeton* grow in the waters of North America. Known also as Floating Brown-leaf, this species bears submerged leaves of a distinctly different shape. Waterfowl eat the fresh shoots and rootstocks and depend extensively on the nut-like fruits, which are produced in abundance and remain attached to the plant into early winter. The long growth season of the plant contributes, in turn, to a lengthened breeding season in northern waters. Much too often the plants are eradicated as part of "good" lake management because they interfere with ease of angling, swimming, and boating. The stylized leaves of this *Potamogeton*, in addition to those of Arrowhead (*Sagittaria,* p. 83), have become popular motifs in artists' depictions of aquatic plant life.

Floating-leaved Pondweed

Each spring the wind brought storms and the wet rains of pollen. Both drifted over the widening thaw of lakes. Lakes of all sizes. Millions of lakes sparkled in the Pleistocene twilight. In early summer we crossed the country of melted ice: horizons of boulder-strewn gravels, glacial till in mounds and ridges, and the long moraines. It all lay scattered like the bones of some beast too huge to imagine.

We came upon a rise and beyond it saw forests like long fingers reaching out, invading. Forests of light and dark spruce, balsam fir, and a scrub of willows. Beyond that was quilted land, patches of pine, birch, and aspen—the coppice that followed fires. Fire and wind and freeze. The forces on the land were physical. We felt the terror of each fierce shaping force. It was a gift simply to endure.

Narrow-leaved Cat-tail
Typha angustifolia / TYPHACEAE

Throughout the world, perhaps no other aquatic plant carries such sum of memory as the common Cat-tail. From drainage ditch and pond to broad lake margin, we can see the brown spikes nodding and hear the dense leaves rustle where redwing blackbirds have called across the April mornings of our lives. Like dragonflies, a memory touches down. In autumn we gather the dark fruits for a fall bouquet. Long before us the dawn tribes fought for user-rights to Cat-tail marshes. Underground stems, or *rhizomes*, make rich flour; so does the golden pollen. The fresh young shoots are eaten like artichoke. Leaves can be woven and dried to shape chair seats, hats, baskets, and mats. Both pollen and tufted fruits are scattered by wind. The species shown here is differentiated from the more widespread *T. latifolia* by its narrower leaves and spikes and the generally smaller stature. It is also the more tolerant of brackish water.

Narrow-leaved Cat-tail

Lakes! Some were old drainage ways dammed by vast moraines. In places the retreating ice stopped, melted, and re-advanced, breaking through old morainal dams, spilling the massive ponded water and flooding the land again like an inland sea. The ancient sluiceways, carved out by those giant floods, lay scattered everywhere across the landscape. We kept our memory of so much water.

In time, all the southern lakes began to die. They dwindled, shrank, filled in, evaporated, year after year under wind and summer sun. They left the landscape mottled, ringed with sediments—*lacustrine* or dark organic soils—muck land with plant debris and in-washed sediments, filling the lakes a foot each century. In other lakes, a foot of sediment might take a thousand years to accumulate. And with drought and the spoils of erosion, lakes can die faster still. Yet, for many lakes, filling takes millennia. From its choppy surface, it is still over thirteen hundred feet to Lake Superior's rocky floor.

Rose-mallow
Hibiscus moscheutos / MALVACEAE

A shrub-like perennial herb, Rose-mallow shares the wind at water's edge with tall reed grasses. This close relative of such common cultivars as Hollyhock and Rose-of-Sharon is known variously as Swamp-mallow, Swamp-rose, and Swamp Rose-mallow, although it bears no relation to the true rose. The flower of Rose-mallow is as striking as any of its family and is also frequently cultivated. The plant tolerates brackish marshes along the eastern coastal plain and extends westward to the wetlands of Indiana and south to the Gulf Coast. It reaches heights of eight feet, with flowers up to eight inches across.

Rose-mallow

The "lake country" is, for the most part, all of the lands north of the Missouri and Ohio Rivers whose valleys were carved out or entrenched by glacial meltwater. Freshly minted land—clear, shining, winter-cold, and geologically young. The ice has been gone little more than one hundred centuries, only twice as long as words have been written.

To the older south, there are quiet waters, too, but fewer and different: swamps and bayous, the great oxbows and sloughs, long chains of dams and human-altered watercourses. Yet, somewhere at the edge of water, earth-wise primal humans have been wearing trails for the last three million years.

Lotus Lily
Nelumbo lutea / NYMPHAEACEAE

The largest, most striking of all our North American aquatic plants, the Lotus Lily has an equally vivid history. The ancient Greek historian Herodotus described a member of this genus common to the Nile. The plant's sun-dried tuberous rootstocks and nut-like fruits yielded flour widely used in baking bread. He related how a few seeds were always rolled in mud, dried, and "cast . . . upon the water," thus proliferating the species. This ancient practice was sufficiently widespread to serve as a metaphor in Ecclesiastes. Native Americans are thought to have disseminated this species extensively because of its value as a food. Children used the large dried fruits as rattles, while the hard, often rounded seeds were objects in a game similar to marbles. The seeds germinate only after being submerged in water and, when collected and kept dry, may remain viable for centuries. Lotus can form dense stands in lakes and sluggish streams where, considered an aggressive weed, it is often eradicated, despite its aesthetic appeal.

Lotus Lily

Making Land

The land was found once more. In time it would be possessed. The Europeans came to stay. They settled, built houses, towns and, above all, made farms. Their great new resource was land. Settlers spoke of "making land," of "letting daylight into the swamp," which meant preparing farmland for tillage.

In the forested east, the physical barriers were a "satanic" trinity of trees and rocks and wet ground. Men looked for special types of forestland and certain kinds of trees that would indicate a particular quality of soil. Soils of good drainage grew hard maple, walnut, and white ash. Such soils could also grow "good corn" and "fit oats" or barley.

Skunk-cabbage
Symplocarpus foetidus / ARACEAE

To those who tramp the wetlands in late winter, the flowering sheath of Skunk-cabbage is a welcome harbinger of longer, warmer light ahead. Its deceitful pollination strategy of attracting flies and gnats to fetid odor, which mimics that of decayed flesh, has caused an abundance of common names referring to smell. One exception refers to the flower's architecture of a hooded *spathe* (large modified bract or leaf) covering a *spadix* (prominent clublike arrangement of flowers) within. The colloquial name Parson-in-a-pillory suggests its well-known family relative, Jack-in-the-pulpit. Despite malodor and an abundance of toxic oxalate crystals, the leaves, if "thrice boiled" in baking soda and salt, are reported to have a pleasant taste. Uncooked, the needlelike crystals provoke intense irritation to mucous membranes. Enthusiasts should carefully distinguish Skunk-cabbage from the poisonous Indian Poke (*Veratrum viride*), which it can resemble and with which it often grows.

Skunk-cabbage

Everywhere men made land. Where the girdled trees stood drooping bark and branches, they called it a "deadening." The first crops were sown with hope under a lattice of dry branches. Winter by winter the dead limbs fell. Farmers stacked the timber about the trunks to facilitate burning.

Other men, more meticulous, perhaps, or wealthier, hired the land cleared outright—all the trees were cut acre by acre, "English" or "Eastern" style. Unless the stumps were pulled as well, sucker sprouts might grow back, some of them twenty feet high in a single year.

Fire was the indispensable tool, and ashes were rich in nutrients. So dead limbs fell, were piled around the dead boles, and all was set ablaze.

Mock Bishop's-weed
Ptilimnium capillaceum / APIACEAE

The delicate foliage of this plant inspired Rafinesque (the nineteenth-century naturalist-professor) to name it "marsh feather" in Greek. The species name repeats this feature of the plant, *capillaceous* meaning pinnately divided or hair-like. The common name derives from the plant's general resemblance to the European Bishop-weed, *Aegopodium podograria,* once a renowned medicinal for gout, hence goutweed. The small white-flowered umbels, characteristic of the Parsley family, appear from mid to late summer. A frequent companion species shown in this picture is the Chair-maker's rush, or Three-square (the distinguishing stem shape), *Scirpus pungens*.

Mock Bishop's-weed

Once the trees were dead in the wet lowlands, swamps, marshes, and wet woods, a strange thing happened, which often went unnoticed. The water table began to rise. Even when the higher "dry-in-June" ground was cleared, the marshes and the swamps and the ponded land began "to grow"—the wetland borders crept uphill.

Few can yet comprehend how much soil-water trees "pump" into the air. Let the forest reclaim a pasture, and its small creek may go dry by midsummer. In autumn, as leaves die, the same rainfall can charge the creek for weeks: the great pump of the forest has shut down.

Purplestem Angelica
Angelica atropurpurea / APIACEAE

This esteemed member of the Parsley family (also known as Cow Parsnip, Alexanders, or Angelica) can, as a young plant, have a lamentable likeness to Poison-hemlock (*Conium maculatum*), the source of the death drug given Socrates. Masterwort, however, is safe to eat, and its leaves (which are considerably larger than those of *Conium*) were widely used as a medicinal—a tea of it being brewed and sipped for influenza or colds or a steaming hot poultice applied to fresh wounds. Native Americans cooked its leafstalks like celery, its young roots like parsnip or rutabaga. Early pioneers gathered "Auntjerichos," as it was known colloquially, with caution and used it as did the Indians. Our species of Angelica is found from Minnesota eastward, south to Illinois and Maryland. It continues to be highly prized as a palatable herb.

Purplestem Angelica

The next most important way to "make land" was to drain the wetlands. Low ground was often rich in nutrients but for crops held too much water or, rather, too little oxygen. Ditches by hundreds, by thousands, crisscrossed the wetlands. On higher ground the tile lines carried more and more water each year to the flood-swollen rivers.

Gradually the surface water tables began to drop. The wetlands began to shrink. The trees were gone and could not hold the surface runoff or intercept soil water. Nutrients were leached away. In time most of the wetlands with crop potential were ditched or tiled or were drained indirectly as the water tables fell.

Common Cursed Crowfoot
Ranunculus sceleratus / RANUNCULACEAE

This wetland species is circumboreal (around the Northern Hemisphere, North America, Europe, and Asia). It extends south to Virginia and Missouri, in the west to New Mexico and California. A member of the Buttercup family, it is called Crowfoot for the splayed shape of its leaves. Some botanists feel that the species epithet—*sceleratus,* meaning "cursed" or "vile"—refers to its habitat; it refers more likely to the plant's high toxic anemonol content. The acrid taste of the leaves successfully discourages most herbivores (unless they are starving), although occasional livestock deaths have been reported.

Common Cursed Crowfoot

Habitat

Water and the nature of its source are ancient symbols to the human mind. The equation is a simple one: without water there is no life. Water contributes 75 percent or more to the weight of most living things, and they die quickly if deprived of it for long. Yet too much water can also be fatal.

The historical meanings of waterways are legion: we first explored the world by following watercourses or by tracking animals that did so. Rivers, lakes, and oceans were the great thoroughfares of discovery and, later, the vital corridors of commerce. And always—after the find, after the risks and losses—we returned as in the old exhortation to dwell in "green pastures . . . beside the still waters." Strange that fresh clean water, so precious to desert peoples, would become inexhaustible in our thinking. And for a brief while, on much of this continent, it was.

Field Mint
Mentha arvensis / LAMINACEAE

Precursor of a taxonomic nightmare, this wetland species is the only mint native to our continent. Years of introducing, cultivating, and naturalizing European species, and much adventive hybridizing left in their wake an almost inscrutable pedigree for the eleven or twelve species described from our region. From juleps to chewing gum, the aromatic nature of such species as Spearmint (*M. spicata*) and Peppermint (*M. piperita*) is well known. The pungent oils that give fresh leaves their minty flavor probably serve to repel a number of insects. Mints are very tenacious when cultivated. Our native Field Mint is itself a circumboreal species and is widespread across the northern two-thirds of the United States.

Field Mint

In the scientific literature on freshwater biology, an old dichotomy separates lakes and streams: the "still" versus the "flowing" waters. To ecologists, aquatic systems are termed, in the logic of Latin, either *lentic* (lake-like) or *lotic* (stream-like).

In living landscapes, however, flowering aquatic plants do not always abide by such distinctions; nor does water itself. Obviously there is a continuum of flow and a great variation in velocity. Water flows into lakes and out again. Rivers overflow into floodplains; the water backs into depressions, into old meander channels, stands for days or weeks, then disappears. A "wetland" implies some prolonged inundation if not a permanent ponding.

Lizard's-tail
Saururus cernuus / SAURURACEAE

Taking its name from its graceful plumes of delicately scented flowers, this is the only species of a single genus of its family (the other one being native to Asia) to grow in our wetlands. The scientific name is from the Greek *saurus* (lizard) and *oura* (tail)—an apt allusion to its drooping, or *cernuus* spike or floral arrangement. Individual flowers have no *perianth* (sepals and petals)—a distinctive feature—and its stamen filaments give the flower its white color. Also called Swamp-lily and Water Dragon, the plant is perennial in wet woods, swamps, oxbows, and shallow open water across eastern North America extending to the Gulf of Mexico. Sold as an ornamental for bog-gardens, it sometimes escapes cultivation and is found growing outside its native range.

Lizard's-tail

The quiet waters familiar to most people are lakes (or reservoirs), ponds, marshes, and swamps. How do they differ? The terms *lake* and *pond* are often used simply to distinguish the size of a body of fresh water; but inevitably there is wide geographic variation in usage. South Branch Pond in Maine's Baxter Park near Mt. Katahdin is not a Midwesterner's prototype of a pond. It is a proper-sized lake.

The distinction between the terms *marsh* and *swamp* is rather more precise, even in popular usage. A swamp contains trees as a prominent feature; a marsh does not. As marshes become shallower, they become wet meadows, sedge meadows, or fens—places where, during much of the year, a hiker might get his boots wet.

Small Yellow Water Crowfoot
Ranunculus gmelinii / RANUNCULACEAE

The *natans* (swimming) form of this species of Water Crowfoot is similar to, but smaller than, the amphibious species Common Cursed Crowfoot (*R. sceleratus*, p. 19). Both plants show a marked *heterophylly* (with floating leaves distinct from the more highly dissected submerged leaves). The splayed leaves give the plants their shared common name, Crowfoot. Growing in cooler waters of North America and Asia, the species was named to honor its discoverer, Johann Gmelin. Several geographic varieties have been described. Shown flowering here, the plant is sharing substrate with Pondweed (*Potamogeton; also see* p. 5) and Sedge (*Carex*).

Small Yellow Water Crowfoot

Among the many types of wetlands, intermittent, ephemeral pools are of supreme importance to myriad species able to carry out brief lifecycles. The ubiquitous roadside ditch is a good example. Wetlands can range, however, from lakes to estuaries to poorly drained and unplowed corners of upland cornfields.

All of the species illustrated in this book inhabit lakes or the wetlands of lake borders. Some of the plants, such as Boneset (p. 27), Joe-Pye weed (p. 31), and Swamp Milkweed (p. 47), are also not uncommon to heavy, wet upland soils of fields and pastures. Included, too, are a few species whose ecological range includes the acid water of bogs, such as Bladderwort (p. 61) and Water-arum (p. 75).

Boneset
Eupatorium perfoliatum / ASTERACEAE

At least sixteen colloquial names designate this distinctive perfoliate plant with its stem that appears to be growing through its leaves (hence the name Throughwort and its corrupted version, Thoroughwort). The latter variant persists, alluding, perhaps, to its widespread and thorough use as a medicine. Boneset, its most common name, may be misconstrued. This was the species of choice by the herbalists for treating a feverish grippe or influenza known variously as bone-break or boneset fever, due to its combination of pain and malaria-type shaking. The plant was also widely prescribed as a diuretic for kidney stones, and its relative (*E. purpureum*) is still called Gravel-root, although more commonly Joe-Pye weed (p. 31). Aguewort, Feverwort, and Sweat-plant are but a few additional herbal names. This species and other Eupatoriums contain the glucoside "eupatorin." References to the plant's efficacy for setting broken bones may be erroneous, though as a general tonic it may have been used by those "with limbs aknittin'."

Boneset

The specific names of these plants often reflect their characteristic habitats, such as *palustra,* meaning "of the swamp" in Latin, and the more obvious *aquaticum, amphibium,* and *natans,* all references to "swimming." Similarly, one of the most important family and genus names is derived from the ancient word for "water nymph"—*Nymphaeaceae* and *Nymphaea*—shown on p. 39. Another, *Potamogeton,* was named from the combination of two Greek words (*potamos* or "river" plus *gaiton* or "neighbor"), giving Pondweed (shown on p. 5) a name meaning "river neighbor."

Marsh Cinquefoil
Potentilla palustris / ROSACEAE

This plant is one of thirty or more species of its genus whose name, *Potentilla* (the diminutive of *potens*), refers to strong medicinal powers attributed to the first-named species *P. Anserina.* The genus characteristically bears palmately compound leaves of five leaflets, hence the common name Five-fingers or (from the Old French) Cinquefoil. A member of the Rose family, it has bright red-to-purple flowers which approach an inch in diameter. The stout perennial stems average two feet in height. Circumboreal in distribution, it is prevalent in inundated ground (wet meadows, swamps, and marshes) south to Indiana, west to California.

Marsh Cinquefoil

ADAPTATIONS

Across the landscape mosaic of wetland sites, only certain specially adapted plants can thrive. Less than 1 percent of the flowering plant species of the world are considered aquatic—fewer than twenty-five hundred. And, if a very strict definition is used, this figure becomes much smaller. The same adaptive traits that allow many plant species to circle a lake may adapt them for a roadside ditch or a flooded cornfield.

The seeds of all truly aquatic plants will survive and germinate in water. And all wetlands have a feature in common which affects a plant's physiology: they are sites where the vital oxygen available to roots and germinating seeds is in short supply. When plants of most species stand for several days or weeks with their roots immersed in water, they die, not as a result of too much water, but rather from too little oxygen. The plants "drown" in the same physiological sense that animals do. It takes plants longer to succumb, however, because most roots can undergo some level of oxygen-free respiration for various periods of time.

Joe-Pye weed
Eupatorium purpureum / ASTERACEAE

Perennial to wet pastures and thickets, as well as stream and lake margins (especially on calcareous soils), this plant has a legendary reputation as a medicinal herb. It is reported that the popularity of this species (also called Spotted Boneset) stems from its wide prescription by the eighteenth-century Native American healer Joseph Pye. His weed, though not known to possess "efficacious curative properties," does belong to a genus that has a significant history. Its common relative, White Snakeroot (*E. rugosum*), when eaten by cows, tainted their milk. Abraham Lincoln's mother, Nancy Hanks, is believed to have died from the "milk sick" when Abe was a young boy living in Indiana. Often epidemic in frontier Midwestern settlements, this illness is now known to have been caused by drinking milk from cows that had grazed on this noxious weed. The plant's technical name is dedicated to the renowned Greek physician Mithridates Eupator, who died in 63 B.C. It blooms from July through late September.

Joe-Pye weed

Aquatic plant species, then, differ from their relatives on well-drained soils in that their roots apparently tolerate a low-oxygen environment. And submerged floating-leaved aquatic plants have developed special conducting systems that transport or diffuse oxygen-rich air between the water surface and the roots.

A plant living in the highly demanding environment of a drowned habitat has one compelling advantage: initially, there is less competition. So, as landscapes evolved, freshwater aquatic sites provided a new area on the earth's surface where solar energy could be captured. It meant that for certain plants substantial changes proved adaptive—the innovations paid off.

It was just the kind of evolutionary invitation that life has invariably accepted. All aquatic flowering plants derive from ones which were originally terrestrial, and they were able to be successful by evolving secondary adaptations to aquatic habit.

Water Smartweed
Polygonum amphibium / POLYGONATUM

This prolific, highly variable, circumboreal aquatic from the Buckwheat family is one of forty-six species of *Polygonum* found in eastern North America. Between fifteen and twenty species are considered to be aquatic. *Polygonum* (many joints) describes the swollen nodes, which are covered by a short sheath called an *ocrea*—all giving the plant a characteristic appearance. Terrestrial members are commonly called Knotweeds, while the aquatics are generally referred to as Smartweeds. Confusingly enough, however, the common barnyard species is frequently referred to by farmers as Smartweed as well. The latter name presumably alludes to the sharp, peppery taste of the leaves. Fresh leaves sparingly diced into a salad make an effective pepper substitute. The abundant fruits are second only to *Potamogeton* (p. 5) as the most important staple for migratory waterfowl. Some fifteen species of ducks are known to depend upon this plant for food.

Water Smartweed

How do the submerged roots of aquatic plants receive sufficient oxygen for respiration? Most of the oxygen used by the submerged parts of an aquatic plant comes from photosynthesis occurring in the leaves. Aquatic plants have retained waxy cuticles on their leaves and, like terrestrial plants, these regulate gas and water loss through special *stomata,* or pores, in the leaf surface. In the leaves of Cat-tail (p. 7), Bur-reed (p. 51), Pickerel-weed (p. 35), and Arrow-arum (p. 45), oxygen concentrations of 20 percent have frequently been measured. Unable to escape the waxy cuticle into the air, the oxygen diffuses downward in the plant, creating an oxygen gradient that extends from the leaves to the submerged lower stem and roots.

Leaves and stems of aquatic plants also have special oxygen-storing cavities, or *lacunae.* This elaborate tissue system of air space is called *aerenchyma,* and it represents one of the most characteristic adaptations of plants to aquatic conditions. In many aquatic plants the internal leaf volume is known to be as much as 70 percent gas space. Such chambers obviously add to buoyancy as well as to oxygen storage capability.

Pickerel-weed
Pontederia cordata / PONTEDERIACEAE

Here the tenacious Pickerel-weed or Wampee curves toward the light among the rushes (*Scirpus*). Common in the east, it extends west to Minnesota and south to Texas, often forming rank growth in shallow ponds and ditches. Its leaves are quite variably shaped but roughly heart-shaped, or *cordate.* The genus is named in honor of a noted eighteenth-century professor from Padua, Guilio Pontedera. From the English name, no doubt, an early correlation was made between this plant and the haunts of the pickerel and other fish. As shown here, once mature, its nut-like seeds are self-planted by recurving *peduncles* (flower stalks), seen also in *Peltandra* (p. 45) and other aquatics. The fruits are an important wildlife staple, especially to swamp deer and muskrat. All parts but the root are edible when properly prepared.

Pickerel-weed

Of equal importance to the aquatic strategy is the presence of a thick cuticle. Its waxy sheen gives the leaves of aquatic plants a characteristic appearance. Water simply beads and runs off the surface. The aquatic Golden-club (*Orontium aquaticum,* p. 37) is also colloquially called Never-wet because of its water-repellent leaves.

In the fall and early winter certain perennial aquatic plants, such as *Utricularia* (p. 61) and *Potamogeton* (p. 5), respond to cold water and altered light by another distinctive type of aquatic adaptation, a special type of asexual propagation. The submerged plants develop winter buds called *turions.* These structures are composed of small masses of undeveloped or aborted leaves, which can break away from the parent plant, float a distance, sink and take root.

Golden-club
Orontium aquaticum / ARACEAE

This early spring flowering plant, whose genus is named for the Syrian river Orontes, is widely grown as an ornamental due to its bright yellow *spadix* from which it derives its most frequent common name, Golden-club. It is also called Bog-torch. Like many other aquatics, it propagates vegetatively by thick *rhizomes,* or rootstocks, growing just beneath the muddy substrate. While found chiefly along the eastern coastal plain from lower New England to Florida and Mississippi, it extends into the Midwest. It is shown here growing with *Potamogeton* (*also see* p. 5) in an Alabama wetland.

Golden-club

Looking back, we can see a pattern in plant evolution. Whenever a severe environment has been encountered, plant groups that exploit it often do so by reverting to some earlier (primitive or arrested juvenile) stage of their development—a phenomenon called *neotony*. While the pattern of inner adaptation is not obvious, we can see many specialized structural adaptations in the Duckweeds and Water-lilies (pp. 41 and 39), for example. These are plant families whose immediate terrestrial ancestors have, apparently, since vanished.

We marvel, and with reason, at such distinctive propriety of niche in the nature of things. The Water-lily family, *Nymphaeaceae* (p. 39), looms alone in exclusive aquatic habit both in nature and in its taxonomic position.

Fragrant Water-lily
Nymphaea odorata / NYMPHAEACEAE

Shown here in early morning light is the Fragrant Water-lily. Flowers last only three or four days and open only in the morning hours. The canoe-shaped petals enhance flotation of the rather large flowers. Following successful pollination, the plant retracts and submerges its peduncles beneath the water where the fruits continue to mature. An adaptive feature, common to several aquatic plants, can be seen here. The under surface of the rounded leaves, or lily pads, develops a deep red-to-purple color. These anthocyanin pigments appear to function both metabolically and protectively. They radiate light back into the green photosynthesizing cells above the red layer, increasing the efficiency of available light, yet shielding leaves from too much sun. The reddish under-leaf trait is diagnostic for this species within its genus. The plant ranges throughout eastern North America, where it is known variously as Sweet-scented Water-lily, Water-cabbage, and Water-nymph and, in the south, Alligator-bonnet. Flower buds were once cooked as a vegetable by Ojibwa Indians.

Fragrant Water-lily

Other plant families and species, unlike the Water-lilies (p. 39) and Duckweeds (p. 41), have preserved their intermediate links and forms. Thus our smallest flowering aquatic genus *Wolffiella* displays an obvious continuity of form with the next smallest, the common *Wolffia*. These tiny plants, called water-meal, are composed of rootless leaves a millimeter or less in diameter, having no vascular development whatsoever. In spite of its size, each small leaf still has stomatal pores and a well-developed waxy cuticle.

A related genus in this same family is the Duckweed (*Lemna*), a somewhat more elaborate plant. *Lemna*, in turn, is structurally similar to the larger Water-flaxseed (*Spirodella*), which has a tiny remnant *spathe*, or hood. And a similarity of chemistry ties all these plants to the Arums (such as Skunk-cabbage, p. 13; Arrow-arum, p. 45; and Sweet-flag, p. 77). These relationships would be quite obscure if the several intermediate forms had become extinct.

Yellow Pond-lily
Nuphar advena / NYMPHAEACEAE

Ranging much farther south than the other *Nuphar* (p. 79), this Pond-lily is tolerant of brackish coastal waters as well. It differs also in having larger leaves with rounded petioles, whereas the leafstalks of Spatterdock (*N. variegata*, p. 79) are decidedly flattened. Cup-like flowers, composed of *tepals* (sepals and petals appearing the same), are slow to open even after *pistils* (female flower parts) are mature; so pollinators enter by crawling over the sticky *stigmas* (parts receptive to pollen grains). Once fertilized, flowers open completely, exposing maturing *stamens* (male flower parts). The plant was used by Native Americans in much the same way as other Pond-lilies. This species is of special significance to much wildlife—muskrat, beaver, porcupine, deer, and a host of ducks. Since it grows prolifically and can crowd out other plants by completely preempting the surface, it has been eradicated from many waterways. The species is shown here with one of our smallest flowering plants, Duckweed (*Lemna minor*).

Yellow Pond-lily

Curiously, in addition to the smallest-leaved plant, one of the largest-leaved plants known to botany is also an aquatic—the tropical *Victoria regia*, or Amazon Lily. Its leaves exceed a meter in diameter, and a single leaf could hold well over a million entire *Wolffia* plants. Among life's familiar contenders, only the insects are as resilient and diverse in their adaptive repertory.

The astonishing degree of structural variability, which aquatic plants exhibit, is called *somatic* (bodily) *plasticity.* Plant organs, such as leaves, can develop in a variety of ways depending upon the influence of growth conditions in a particular environment. In species such as the Water Crowfoot (pp. 25 and 43), the submerged leaves are narrower and more highly dissected than the emergent leaves.

Experimentation has shown that carbon dioxide concentration greatly affects leaf shape. Underwater, leaves accumulate carbon dioxide and are often marginally deficient in oxygen. The same effect on leaf forms has been observed out of water in experiments in which the carbon dioxide concentrations have been elevated.

Yellow Water Crowfoot
Ranunculus flabellaris / RANUNCULACEAE

With its leaves hidden beneath the water, this familiar amphibious Crowfoot extends its buttercup-yellow flowers among new leaves of Cat-tail (*also see* p. 7). The species frequents quiet waters and muddy shores across the United States from North Carolina to Louisiana, west to California and northward. It is shown here in the shallow water of a northern Illinois lake where the plant's flowers are at anthesis in late May. The species name *flabellaris* (fan-like) refers to the shape of the plant's much-dissected leaves. Pliny (the ancient Roman scholar who authored the celebrated *Historiae Naturalis* during the first century) applied the name *Ranunculus* (little frog) to this genus whose aquatic species share the frogs' habitats.

Yellow Water Crowfoot

In planting and protecting their seeds, aquatic plants display a number of modifications, all bent to a similar goal. In plants such as Lotus Lily (*Nelumbo*, p. 11), Fragrant Water-lily (*Nymphaea*, p. 39), Floating-heart (*Nymphoides*, p. 53), Pondweed (*Potamogeton*, p. 5), and Arrow-arum (*Peltandra*, p. 45), to name just a few, a dramatic change occurs.

Following fertilization, a hormone believed to come from the embryo causes the peduncle to curve, coil, or collapse and submerge the fruit. The fruits do not normally break open. Gradually the woody encasement (involving much stem tissue) must partially decay before the hard, stony seed (often including the *endocarp*, or inner wall of the fruit) is released. Some seeds have a gelatinous coat that imbibes water and swells until the seeds are forcibly ejected. This can be aided by a similar swelling of the mucilage of the inner fruit wall.

Arrow-arum
Peltandra virginica / ARACEAE

This plant is another member of the Arum family, which includes Skunk-cabbage (p. 13), Golden-club (p. 37), and Duckweed (*Lemna minor*), with which it is growing here. It also bears a distinct resemblance to Arrowhead (*Sagittaria*, p. 83), although Arrow-arum blooms much earlier. (The two aquatic plants can further be distinguished by their leaf venation: *Peltandra*'s veins run diagonally outward from the midrib while *Sagittaria*'s are parallel to it.) Also called Tuckahoe or Green-arrow, the Arrow-arum displays the same kind of protective self-planting common to many aquatic plant species: the fruit's peduncle bends over and submerges its gelatinous-coated seeds. Seeds of this aquatic are eaten by waterfowl and its roots were pounded into flour by Native Americans. This is a familiar eastern species but is also common to shallow water from Nova Scotia far west to Oregon and south from Texas to North Carolina.

Arrow-arum

The long lakeshore of early spring or late autumn is a place of winds. With little warning, winds may swing in from the southeast, north, or east and churn the whitecaps leeward in gusty squalls. Aquatic plants have met the challenge of a sum of factors, and they differ from their terrestrial ancestors with respect to wind as well as to water. While their aquatic habit is a secondary adaptation, so too is their relationship to the wind. (The term *secondary* here means that the immediate ancestral groups of these plants possessed different adaptations.)

Many important aquatic flowers that are now wind-pollinated, such as Cat-tail (p. 7) and Bur-reed (p. 51), are descended from insect-pollinated forms. (Many of these flowers still retain *vestigial nectaries,* or rudimentary nectar-producing organs.) Fruit and seed dispersal may also show a reversion to wind dispersal.

Yet, many insect-pollinated species also exploit the wind to scatter their fruits. Examples of these are Joe-Pye weed (p. 31) and Swamp Milkweed (p. 47). There is obviously similarity between buoyancy in air and buoyancy in water.

Swamp Milkweed
Asclepias incarnata / ASCLEPIADACEAE

Swamp Milkweed is one of the twenty eastern North American species of this widespread genus. The generic name honors the Greek god of medicine, son of Apollo, who had been taught the art of healing; the specific name refers to the flesh-red color of the flowers. As in all milkweeds, a white latex exudes from the broken stems; hence the common name. The flower's architecture—five *stamen* tips that have fused into a broad disk above the two ovary *styles,* bewildering many a beginning botany student—serves as an effective pollen-trapping structure. The fruit pods are edible when immature and are prepared like okra; unopened flower buds may be cooked like broccoli. Roots, leaves, and late summer stems are toxic, however, and were the source of an early cathartic medicine. Yet Monarch caterpillars eat this plant voraciously; they (and the butterflies they become) are themselves poisonous to potential predators. The plant is found abundantly in wet meadows and marshes from Manitoba to New Mexico and eastward to Maine and Florida.

Swamp Milkweed

These secondary wind strategies make evolutionary sense around northern lakes that are wind-rich and pollinator-poor. In such areas a short growth season selected for earlier flowering times, thus allowing an ample span for a complete life cycle before the killing frosts. Winter too often did not wait for the finely timed, coevolved plant-insect patterns to the south. The evolving northern wetlands were being shaped by wind and water and cold, as the lengthening summers were wearing the ice away.

Swamp Thistle
Cirsium muticum / ASTERACEAE

This vivid flower of autumn wetlands is a surprisingly delicate and harmless thistle. *Muticum* (without points) describes the relatively unarmed leaves, which are usually quite spiny in others of this genus. Dioscorides (the ancient Greek physician who wrote *De Materia Medica,* the leading text on pharmacology for some sixteen centuries) named the genus *Cirsium,* from the ancient Greek for thistle. It is a biennial, producing only a basal rosette during the first year. The under-leaf surface is densely woolly. Its second-year flower heads are borne on long stems having few leaves. Common to the eastern United States and Canada, this species ranges south to Tennessee and northern Louisiana. A related thistle is the national flower of Scotland.

Swamp Thistle

Succession

How often we have rowed or paddled shoreward from open water and entered an old continuum of change unknowingly. Offshore, in the clear, still-open water, rooted submerged plants suddenly appear toward the shallows: Tape Grasses, Coon-tail, and Bladderwort (p. 61).

We then come through a zone of floating leaves. The vegetation that rings lakes and ponds, marshes and swamps, forms distinct zones and is most clearly seen in the succession from Water-lilies (p. 39) and Pondweed (p. 5) to the emergent plants such as Bur-reed (p. 51) and Cat-tail (p. 7). Beyond this band of aquatic or amphibious species, we paddle through a shrub zone of Buttonbush (p. 89), willow, or alder, with saplings of the wet-ground forest being the last to come into view.

This series of zones is a developmental (successional) sequence. As lakes or ponds fill, the fringes converge centripetally. The "eye" of open water closes, almost a blink in geologic time. Now a swamp forest thrives. The centuries close in, bringing wave on wave of more mesic species, herbs, and trees. Ecologists call the whole of this succession a *hydrosere*. A pervasive phenomenon, it happens everywhere there is water.

Bur-reed
Sparganium eurycarpum / SPARGANIACEAE

Like its common order relative *Typha* (p. 7), Bur-reed has a distinctive, highly modified floral arrangement on the upper stem. As shown here, separate unisexual flowers are arranged in dense clusters, with the male inflorescences developing toward the upper ends of the zigzagged branched stalks. As the pistillate clusters develop into packed and hardened seed-like fruits, the burs or male flowers are shed. The tall sheath-leaves and the rhizome growth habit have a marked resemblance to Cat-tail. Both plants provide superior cover for numerous waterfowl and stabilize and build new substrate. The fruits of Bur-reed and its starchy rhizome are an important food for many wildlife species.

Bur-reed

Originally, a hydrosere was described as the changing physiognomic pattern of an aquatic community that the human eye and mind perceives. Such structural change was apparent to keen observers who compared one place with another. The term *forest succession* was coined by the author-naturalist Henry David Thoreau. He encountered this phenomenon everywhere around Concord—across the abandoned farmlands and cutover woods of New England. He saw it along Walden Pond.

Such visible structural changes reveal vital and complex functions. Subtle changes in process rates and the balances toward which each change is tending are affected by many things: oxygen availability, organic content, sediment load, light penetration, temperature, and acidity; also, rates and manner of decay and, most importantly, the rates of nutrient release.

It is these first-order changes that orchestrate the tempo and the pattern of succession. The scenario can take millennia. Yet it is possible to span such a drama in seconds by casually walking the length of a weathering pier. A *sere* (an orderly progression of community change) can exist as zones in space as well as in stages of time.

Floating-heart
Nymphoides cordata / MENYANTHACEAE

This aquatic member of the Gentian family is frequently confused with the true Water-lilies (*Nymphaea*, p. 39). It is one of two native species assigned to its genus, with a third species (*N. peltata*) introduced from Europe. The species name, *cordata*, suggests its typically heart-shaped leaves that, with the plant's small white flowers, resemble a small water-lily (the literal meaning of the genus name). Flower clusters are borne and develop beneath the water. There is a secondary elongation of the flower-bearing stems up to the water surface as the flowers mature. This allows for pollination above the water, yet protects the submerged immature flowers. Normally, a ring of adventitious roots develops from the stem (or *petiole*) just below the flower cluster. A perennial, the plant propagates vegetatively in shallow water by stout branching rhizomes imbedded in the substrate.

Floating-heart

Events in aquatic succession can be shaped by conditions below the surface. A meter or so beneath the sun-flecked, wind-furrowed water along the shores of northern lakes, the sediments churn and shift—coarse sands, light gravels—tumbling in the steady wash of waves. Up the lake margin, a stream enters, depositing a fan of silt and clay. The steady stream-flow creates a countercurrent, and, to either side, a silt bar is built. Here, reeds or rushes can take root and a fringe of plants spreads out and forms a fragile barrier. Among the reeds the wave action is gradually broken; sediments accumulate and stabilize. Now other plants can follow the pioneers—invading, living, dying, adding organic matter—further slowing the waves and accumulating sediment. The process spreads—a foot, a yard, year after year.

Then comes a year of violent winter storms few winter-hardy residents can even remember. The storm flood obliterates the shoreline under eight-, ten-, twelve-foot waves which rip old piers away; the vegetated mud bars, reed marshes, and beaches—all disappear. Then by midsummer, the slow relentless process of invasion begins once again: grain by grain, seed by seed—the old tenacity of leaf and root driven by the sun.

Swamp-loosestrife
Lysimachia thyrsiflora / PRIMULACEAE

Amid stalks of Bulrush, stems of Swamp-loosestrife crowd muddy ground deep in a Wisconsin swamp. Both the common and generic names describe the legendary attributes of this plant as a medicinal. Ancient physicians, English herbalists and frontier doctors alike furthered the use of a tonic made from this plant for its ability to soothe nervous conditions. Colonial farmers even fed the herb to yokes of oxen believing that this would pacify the animals into working together more harmoniously. Presumably much was sold, but the plant's efficacy for the "loss of strife" is less certain. Juice from the plant was also used to bleach hair and provide relief from skin irritations. This species is found throughout the northern parts of North America, Europe, and Asia. It grows south as far as New Jersey and Missouri. Some taxonomists assign this particular Loosestrife to the genus *Naumburgia* for technical reasons.

Swamp-loosestrife

In smaller lakes where the water is less roiled, a different pattern can occur, and events may move more rapidly. Cat-tails (p. 7) may emerge quickly in shallow water. Their plumed fruits (*pappus achenes*) are delivered continuously across long distances—brought along on legs and feathers of ducks and wading birds. Once a few Cat-tails are established, wind and water scatter the fruits each year. Cat-tail, quick to colonize, spreads like a weed. The Duckweeds and Beggar-ticks (pp. 57 and 85), likewise, are highly vagile and move about rapidly by hitchhiking on the "skirts" of shorebirds and waterfowl. Each season, more and different kinds of plants arrive. Such aquatic communities appear to develop as a function of time, proximity to seeds, and means of dissemination.

Beggar-tick
Bidens laevis / ASTERACEAE

In the low wet soils of the upper Midwest, this Beggar-tick may bloom into early winter. Though it is quite similar to *B. cernua* (p. 85), the flowering heads of Beggar-tick remain erect as fruits mature. The plant is known from New Hampshire to Florida, and west to Illinois, growing in marshes and in the margins of pools and sluggish streams, in either fresh or brackish water. It occurs again on the Pacific Coast and is also recorded in South America. The plant is sometimes called Smooth Bur-marigold, distinguishing it from the Nodding Bur-marigold.

Beggar-tick

Succession is simple in concept, yet complex in reality. The number of interrelationships is enormous and in their totality are, no doubt, beyond our complete comprehension. But we can talk about trends and examples.

Over the years we have watched extensive aquatic communities develop in the borrow pits beside the interstate highways. Life does not care how such shallow lakes are formed. The scenario is much the same: a plant species invades; a pioneer plant provides effective cover for a visiting bird; another may serve as a food source. Other plants, newly arrived, may provide nesting sites and nest-building materials. The visiting birds inadvertently introduce new plant competitors. With dense population growth, the birds may proliferate parasites and weaken the species population. While numbers may decline, more animal species arrive—insects, amphibians, and fishes. The herbivores, or plant grazers, now attract carnivores on a regular basis—marsh hawk and mink. Fish life diversifies and thrives. The lake community becomes more stratified as life cycles partition space and time in a strategy of definite zones and seasons.

Swamp-candles
Lysimachia terrestris / **PRIMULACEAE**

Instead of flowers, this member of the Primrose family often produces asexual bulbets in certain leaf-axils. Linnaeus (the famous eighteenth-century Swedish botanist) first described a vegetatively propagating plant of this species, but he mistook it for terrestrial Mistletoe. Also called Yellow or Bog Loosestrife, the common name Swamp-candles is quite appropriate to the bright yellow floral array shown here. Its habitat includes old fields, wet woods, and thickets, as well as the banks of lakes and ponds and in cranberry bogs in the east.

Swamp-candles

Finally, as long, complex yet flexible food chains grow and develop into webs, it becomes possible for an increasing diversity of animal species to rear young, as food, cover, and nesting sites develop. The submerged carnivorous Bladderworts (p. 61) may be present now, their modified pouch-like leaf-traps consuming nitrogen-rich prey such as *Daphnia*, the water flea. Every liter of water is alive with hundreds of species of small organisms—a viable microcosm of energy transformations winding down deep through chains of light and life. Rain upon rain, in spring and fall, death's debris is ever drifting downward. Through the sediment-blurred water, the fate of the lake is clear.

Bladderwort
Utricularia cornuta / LENTIBULARIACEAE

Supporting these emergent flowers is a nutritional apparatus unique among our submerged-stem aquatics. Among the dissected, photosynthesizing leaves of this carnivorous species are many modified leaf-bladders, each an intricately constructed animal-trapping device. Its secretions attract microscopic invertebrates; small crustacean animals, such as water fleas (*Daphnia*); and various small larvae (including those of mosquito) into the triggered death-pouches. Exuded enzymes digest the victims, liberating their usable nitrogen—an element that is generally in very low supply in the acidic waters where this plant most frequently grows. The species is found from Newfoundland to Minnesota, south to Texas and Florida.

Bladderwort

Resilience

Our understanding of nature's ecological workings is historically rooted in technical studies of structural and taxonomic developments. More recent studies focus on the functions of biotic communities and, more specifically, on energy flow and on cycling of nutrients within a community or ecological system. In the story of aquatic habitats, there is a special legacy to recount. Relatively few scientific investigations warrant the designation "milestone"; however, one such study of the lake as an ecosystem has substantially affected the direction of a new science.

Southern-blue Iris
Iris virginica / IRIDACEAE

Known variously as Blue-flag or Fleur-de-lis (the flower stylized as the armored emblem of heraldry), this species is described by some botanists as a northern variety (*I. shrevei*) of Southern Blue-flag (*I. virginica*). It is, however, more branched and develops longer fruits. Common to swampy woods and wet meadowlands, the plant shows a familiar strategy of aquatic plants in the peduncle that recurves and becomes prostrate as the fruit matures under water. Shown here amid various ferns, the species can form dense colonies from the growth of stout rhizomes.

Southern-blue Iris

In the early 1940s, Raymond Lindeman, a young ecologist, studied a Minnesota lake—Cedar Creek Bog Lake. His study attempted to synthesize several old and new ways of thinking about processes at work in aquatic communities by looking at food chains and energy flows. This focus on what he called the "trophic dynamic aspect" generated further understanding about food relationships and their interdependency as well as the overall patterns of energy allocation within lakes and other systems. Lindeman's scientific contribution and the tradition from which it grew proved to be a base for a chain of intellectual energy-flow concepts and hypotheses on the nature of ecosystems.

Swamp Lousewort
Pedicularis lanceolata / SCROPHULARIACEAE

Folklore accounts remain divided as to whether livestock grazing colonies of this plant became covered with lice, or whether the plant helped repel lice and similar pests once the animals became infested. In any case, the genus name, *Pedicularis*, applied centuries ago, is from the Latin word for "louse." Curiously, the plant itself is a partial parasite, often on grass roots, where fungal threads help supply it with nutrients. The bilaterally symmetrical flowers, typical of the Snapdragon family, are arranged in "pinwheel" fashion on a floral spike. This striking feature makes Swamp Lousewort unmistakable in the field, where it can easily be spotted during summer months, growing in areas of fresh water—along lake shores and spring branches, in wet meadows and fens.

Swamp Lousewort

Energy flows and food chains become food webs, as the lake grows older, more complex, and more stable. Aquatic plants, from macrophytes to microscopic algae, form the basis for many natural food chains. The fruits of many species and, especially, their seeds, provide food for waterfowl and mammals. Insects, snails, and mammals graze leaves and shoots. The fruits, rhizomes, and roots are eaten by birds and mammals, including man. Epiphytic algae growing on submerged stems are grazed by minute animals such as crustaceans and the larvae of insect multitudes. The larvae are the source of energy for minnows and small sunfish. Larger predatory fish such as bass and pike, in turn, harvest these. Here and there this food chain ends with a Mepps spinner or daredevil spoon and a frying pan.

Watercress
Rorippa nasturtium-aquaticum / BRASSICACEAE

This edible aquatic cress is a perennial European species of the Mustard family that has naturalized widely in this country. It is well known for its use as a salad garnish, collected in early spring when its leaves are most palatable. By early summer, the leaves have become quite peppery from the accumulation of various metabolic salts and acids, including calcium oxalate. This popular salad green grows best in clear, often spring-fed streams and pools. However, the plant does tolerate rather badly polluted water and, in any event, should be washed thoroughly before eating. As in other aquatics, epiphytic organisms (such as algae, bacteria, water shrimp, sow bugs, and larvae) grow on the stems and leaves, making the plant important to certain food chains.

Watercress

One of the most important food chains starts with death: detritus and detritivores. Each year the dead vegetation accumulates—discarded leaves and stems and dead animals. Bacteria and water molds begin the breakdown process. And so the food chains persist, as does the long continuum of life.

Wetlands are one of the earth's vast feeding grounds and a great natural nursery where life can hatch and thrive. Given these rich natural subsidies—water and light, fresh air and nutrients—life inexorably finds a way.

Water-plantain
Alisma subcordatum / ALISMATACEAE

Alisma belongs to one of the most primitive of the flowering plant families; more than fifty species of the family are aquatic. Many botanists believe that monocots such as lily and orchid share an ancestral lineage with this group. The family *Alismataceae* has characteristics that indicate a possible evolutionary connection of the monocotyledons with the dicotyledonous family *Ranunculaceae*. The species shown here is circumboreal, being indigenous to shallow water and wet ground across the Northern Hemisphere, although some authorities consider the European species to be distinctive from our own. Water-plantain has broad ecological amplitude and ranges as far south as Florida and Mexico. The plant has had various purported medicinal uses, from treating hydrophobia to kidney stones. Its plantain-like leaf accounts for both its common and scientific names.

Water-plantain

Normally for such habitats, the supply of nutrients and their rate of release are the master factors—too little or too much and the system starts to fail. Biologists speak of minima, maxima, optima: too much nutrient overfeeds and, in the end, aerobic decay bacteria exhaust the oxygen supply for higher life forms. This phenomenon, called *eutrophication,* is increased wherever excess fertilizer is leached from farmlands or comes downstream from domestic sewage outfalls. It also occurs naturally as lakes slowly fill in. In such shallow dying lakes, a severe winter or thick ice can snuff out the last schools of fish in a single season.

Ragged Fringed Orchid
Habenaria lacera / ORCHIDACEAE

This wide-ranging Ragged Fringed Orchid, having several varieties and hybrids, is found on both dry and wet sites. One of the most common species of its genus, it grows principally in wet woods or open, sunny marshes. It is shown here with fern and rush, growing in a Massachusetts swamp. The genus name is from *habena* (thong or rein), which presumably alludes to the shape of the floral spur in some species. As to the origin of the species epithet: the corolla lip appears torn, or lacerated. Many taxonomic manuals now list this species as *Platanthera lacera,* but Gleason and Cronquist follow the traditional name. The plant flowers from mid to late summer and early into autumn.

Ragged Fringed Orchid

Let us assume that a particular area receives thirty inches of rainfall a year—an approximate average were all parts of North America to receive equal portions. What is the fate of this water?

Were we to think of water in terms of these thirty inches, twenty-one inches would return, rather quickly, to clouds by evaporation and the transpiration of plants. Part of that amount replenishes and keeps the water balance in living things, and so sustains the biosphere. The remaining nine inches would travel to the sea or recharge aquifers.

Along its journey, man would use three inches, on average, in some manner. Three inches in thirty are sufficient to help power an industrial society—from turbines to chemical reactors. Three inches are enough to process a nation's sewage and laundry, quench its thirst, water its golf courses, and extinguish the midnight fires.

Buckbean
Menyanthes trifoliata / MENYANTHACEAE

A close relative of the more familiar Gentian, this genus has but a single species, which occurs around the boreal circle from Europe and Asia to North America. It ranges south through the Midwest to Missouri. The plant and the flower's delicate architecture were first described by Theophrastus (the Aristotelian Greek philosopher who wrote extensively on plants). He observed the slow sequential opening of the *raceme inflorescence* (floral arrangement with flowers along an axis), thus naming the plant *Menyanthes* from *meny* (disclosing or revealing) and *anthos* (flower). Its distinctive three-segmented leaf-blade explains the species epithet and also the confusion of the common name as a "bean" because of the similarity of the leaves to those of legumes. An older name was Goat's-bean, giving rise to the speculation that the French for goat (*bouc*) tells us why the plant is often called *Buck*bean. The white petals are bearded and may be tinged pink.

Buckbean

"Running water purifies itself every ten miles." This was a common and reasonably accurate assumption during most of nineteenth-century America. Yet today, in the course of human use, water collects certain things, seen and unseen, that were not there before. Municipal drinking water contains many different human-contributed molecules that were not in the original rainfall. Hundreds of different synthetic chemical substances have been identified from supposedly fresh waters used domestically across the country. And the numbers have grown steadily. They include a plethora of radioactive wastes; compounds from prescription drugs; cyanide; and such heavy metals as mercury, lead, and cadmium. Most of this effluent has not been a part of the aquatic environment until recently.

Like much of the rest of the earth, aquatic habitats are an ongoing evolutionary experiment. There are questions as to how resilient wetland plant species are to the metabolic insult of such novel chemistry from our "effluent society," and what is or will be the final cost. Overtly and inadvertently, the coming generations will experience the answer.

Water-arum
Calla palustris / ARACEAE

The only species in its genus, Water-arum is typically a far northern (circumboreal) plant growing in cold bogs and swamps. Also called Wild-calla, Water-dragon, Swamp Robin, and Water Lily, it looks much like the Calla Lily of Eastertide, but these two plants do not belong to the same genus and neither of them are true lilies, though the misnomers persist. The fame of Water-arum as a bread-food appears to have originated with Linneaeus's account of its use in Scandinavia. Both the roots and the seed were ground into flour and dried for a period of days to rid them of the acrid and peppery taste caused by needle-like crystals of calcium oxalate, a characteristic of the family *Araceae*, which includes Skunk-cabbage (p. 13), Sweet-flag (p. 77), and Jack-in-the-pulpit. Pollination of the plant's white flowers, borne on long stalks, is aided by water snails as well as by insects.

Water-arum

Allowed the gift of time for succession and evolution, the resilience of life is truly awesome. How often we sense it. There are now reports of bacteria that *depend* on antibiotics! For many years, men have waged war against certain aquatic plants that have been considered weeds—Cat-tail (p. 7), Water-lily (p. 39), Lizard's-tail (p. 23), Sweet-flag (p. 77), and Bulrush, to name just a few.

For some people, the plants are simply a nuisance to recreation, including boating, fishing, and swimming. For certain kinds of wildlife management, Cat-tail and Sweet-flag are of concern since they tend to choke out Wild Rice and Pickerel-weed (p. 35), plants that are especially beneficial to waterfowl, particularly game ducks.

Sweet-flag
Acorus calamus / ACORACEAE

This flag-like member of a family closely related to the arums is widely known by at least nineteen different common names, among them Sweet Cane, Sweet Root, Calamus, Sweet Rush, and Cinnamon Sedge. Forming dense stands resembling Cat-tail (p. 7), plants can reach six feet in height. Common to borders of quiet waters in North America, it is also found throughout Europe and Asia. While the leaves are toxic, its underground stem, or *rhizome,* is palatable when boiled. Early settlers made a gingery candy from the rhizomes and the same aromatic portion was dried and used by colonial women in sachets. And leaves were often strewn on floors to give homes a pleasant smell—hence the many common names referring to its sweetness. Mentioned four times in the Bible, Calamus was highly valued along with frankincense and myrrh. Bundles of rhizomes are sometimes still sold in quaint pharmacies.

Sweet-flag

Removal! The Water-lilies (p. 39) and Spatterdocks (p. 79) went first: cut, raked, and hauled mechanically. Severe cases might warrant a week of dredging. Waterways were channelized, the banks cut vertically and too deep for easy re-rooting. Other plants proved more tenacious, so chemicals were used—first, sodium arsenate. It worked, and it was cheap. A dime's worth would do the job. It was so effective that it would leave the substrate sterile for several years.

Some species, however, seemed to defy such eradication. Certainly not from affection was Water Hyacinth (the introduced aquatic plant from Africa) dubbed "the million dollar weed"! Efforts to remove or even control the spread of this family relative of our common Pickerel-weed (p. 35) in many important waterways of the south have reached staggering costs. In casual removal efforts, chopping up the plants simply enhanced their spread since each fragment could initiate a new colony. To empty a niche is to invite invasion.

Variegated Spatterdock
Nuphar variegata / **NYMPHAEACEAE**

One of ten species of a genus found throughout the Northern Hemisphere, the plants are variously known as Cow Lily, Bullhead Lily, Pond-collard and, in eastern Canada, as Pied-de-cheval (foot-of-the-horse), describing the shape of the floating leaves. A common aquatic, it grows along pond margins and in slow streams from Labrador to Alaska, and south to Indiana. It propagates vegetatively by prolific rhizomes, which were used extensively by the northern Indians, who often stole them from muskrat lodges. Seeds were also gathered and ground into flour or roasted until they popped like corn. New flowers of a colony are emerging here at the edge of a Cat-tail stand in a Wisconsin lake.

Variegated Spatterdock

But other "non-target" forms of life were poisoned, too. Trout died in water having 0.14 parts of sodium arsenate per million. Curiously, carp succumbed at 0.3 while sunfish, including bass, survived at up to 2 parts per million. Sodium chlorate was also effective and less dangerous as a toxin, but it would occasionally explode. Copper sulfate has become a standard chemical for removal, and it still is widely used. At rates of a pound or so per million gallons of water, one may rid a lake of excessive algal growth and certain larger "weeds." It works especially well on a hot day when the plants are under stress. When eutrophication occurs, plant overgrowth poses a nearly intractable problem to lake management.

With the effectiveness of our modern chemical arsenal, however, coupled with dredging, drainage, and pollution, it has become in many areas a far more difficult problem to save the dwindling natural habitats of native aquatic plants.

Water-pennywort
Hydrocotyle umbellata / APIACEAE

Most common to the wet, open areas of the eastern coastal plain, Water-pennywort has an intriguing disjunct occurrence in an area around the southeastern toe of Lake Michigan. It is found again on the west coast and in tropical America—a challenge to plant geographers. The minute flower umbels are rather inconspicuous among the rounded *peltate,* or centrally stalked leaves. The genus name means "water-cup." Like various other round-leaved species, the common epithet, pennywort, is used. The plant is also called Marsh or Indian Pennywort, and Navelwort.

Water-pennywort

Epilogue

In ecology, it is function that shapes the meaning of things and events. Wetlands, swamps, lakes, and marshes—these are habitats of vast and myriad functions, of immense and intricate meanings. We stand on a lake shore, looking across the margin of Arrowhead (p. 83) and Cat-tail (p. 7), across Reed and Spatterdock (p. 79). There is something reflected and to reflect upon—sunlight on the water, flecks of shadow, algae, minute animals, plankton—all are merging in a vast journey of energy. The energy flows, moves on into longer and darker shadows, which disappear into the darkness beyond the lily pads. There is something here that we understand—the whole of it—tenacious, intact, and resilient. Only the images that we extract are fragile. Water is filled with life. It is as vital as the blood that moves across our brain, alive and burning the fuels of perception.

We stand among mosquitoes and black flies, ankle-deep in mud. All that is "out there," all that we see at *that* moment, suddenly has found its way into a unique existence through the evolved molecular energy of the human mind.

Arrowhead
Sagittaria latifolia / ALISMATACEAE

Swamp Potato and Duck Potato are both colloquial names applied to Arrowhead. The plant, with arrowhead-shaped (*sagittate*) leaves, was mentioned by Lewis and Clark as an important staple of several Native American tribes. It produces abundant starchy tubers, which the Chinooks of the Pacific Northwest called Wapato. Indians often gathered the tubers with their feet while wading and routinely raided muskrat lodges to get at the large stores muskrats had put there for the winter. Women boiled the tubers and strung them to dry as they did wild apples and other fruits. Primarily a temperate zone species, its broad range is trans-Canadian, south to Mexico and east to Florida. In the Midwest, the plants may flower continuously from June through September.

Arrowhead

It does not really matter to aquatic life how a particular lake was formed. For a plant's purpose, a lake left by a glacier or an earthquake or an old meander might as well have been fashioned by the Corps of Engineers or the TVA or a farmer's backhoe. In each case, through an inexorable process, the water becomes an ecological and evolutionary home, however brief.

We also know that in order to have something resembling a kettle-hole lake south of the glacial border, you must dig it yourself. Even to the north, lakes fill and die naturally. What difference does it make? Why save a *natural* lake or marsh or swamp? Why not construct a new one, design and engineer it in elaborate detail to whatever we wish? It *is* possible!

But, beyond the looming matter of cost and the ghost of natural economy, something deep within us today—an almost alien part—objects. The objection is more like something felt or heard—a sound or an echo that is almost inaudible to contemporary culture. Yet it haunts us. And it speaks a "No" to technology's "Yes."

Nodding Bur-marigold
Bidens cernua / ASTERACEAE

With fruits far more familiar to most people than its flower, this plant is called Bur-marigold, Beggar-tick, Pitchforks, and Sticktight. It no doubt has other common epithets coined by those removing the two-pronged fruits (burs) by the hundreds from socks and trousers in October! The name *Bidens* means "two-teeth," and the tiny recurved barbs on these two-fruited extensions effectively disperse it. *Cernua* means "nodding"—an appropriate autumnal metaphor for the end of a season.

Nodding Bur-marigold

This notion of "the natural" keeps welling up from deep within our thinking. It seems more akin to the flow of our lives, like a spring, a source, and it can crest suddenly like a stream at flood time. It moves swiftly with force against the idea of so total a human manipulation of the earth—of more channelization, more filled lakes, more drainage. It rages at all the human-fashioned, human-fettered, human-plundered, human-simplified things that can trash a landscape. This part of us, the ancient survivor, wants wildness or its vestige. It remembers. Surely some things must be left as they are and were; must be allowed simply to rise and fall with the seasons of their being. We sense it is natural, like life itself. It is that part in all of us that would be "free."

Above the compelling chatter of cost-effective logic, we hear another sound. It is this "other" we want. In the end, there is no articulation of its reason. We only know of the frame of the human puzzle, a gift, an edge. Ultimately, wildness holds the measure of all that is human. Were the last of it to vanish, *human* is a word we would no longer need. There would be no "other."

Cardinal-flower
Lobelia cardinalis / CAMPANULACEAE

Our only red Lobelia and perhaps our most vivid native fall-flowering plant, Cardinal-flower is infrequently found and appears on many lists of endangered species. Its rarity is, in part, due to its unique floral architecture that depends on the autumnal activity of hummingbirds for pollination. Despite the fact that it is bilaterally symmetrical, the flower lacks a sufficient "landing platform" for cosmopolitan bees (none is required by the birds). Several botanists recognize that the range and frequency of the species reflect the relative abundance of hummingbirds in late summer. Its genus name honors the sixteenth-century Flemish herbalist Matthias de l'Obel. Both the common and technical species names allude to the deep yet vivid red of church cardinals' cassocks, and this, then, ties the floral color to the name of our familiar redbird.

Cardinal-flower

The many conflicts over land use hold an intrinsic bias against preservation. It is in the nature of the conflict that "developers" need win only once. Preservationists must do battle again and again and again for the same objective. The exceptions are the few deliberate programs to preserve wetlands and other natural areas in which land, once dedicated, is safe for a future generation—a generation that will also have a choice for the context of its own evolutionary odyssey.

Buttonbush
Cephalanthus occidentalis / RUBIACEAE

Lakes die. In their quiet going, an invasion of shrubs and trees begins. Among the several pioneer shrub species is the familiar Buttonbush, a dark-wooded perennial known in the Quebec lake country simply as Bois Noir. *Cephale* (head) and *anthos* (flower) describe its conspicuous spherical inflorescence. It is the one species of its genus found in the Western Hemisphere, hence its specific name, *occidentalis*. Throughout much of its range in North America, its foliage and twigs may be browsed by deer and beaver; its nut-like achenes are a staple for ducks and rail. The plant is seen here at land's edge, where its prolific growth portends the end of this shallow lake.

Buttonbush

Suggestions for Further Reading

Barnes, R. S. K., and K. H. Mann. 1991. *Fundamentals of Aquatic Ecology.* 2nd ed. Boston: Blackwell Scientific Publications. (Rev. ed. of *Fundamentals of Aquatic Ecosystems,* 1980.)

Brock, Thomas D. 1985. *A Eutrophic Lake: Lake Mendota, Wisconsin.* New York: Springer-Verlag.

Cowardin, L. M., V. Carter, F. C. Golet, and E. T. LaRoe. 1979. *Classification of Wetlands and Deepwater Habitats of the United States.* Washington, D.C.: U.S. Department of the Interior, Fish and Wildlife Service, 131 pp.

Crow, Garrett E., C. Barre Hellquist, and Norman C. Fassett. 2000. *Aquatic and Wetland Plants of Northeastern North America: A Revised and Enlarged Edition of Norman C. Fassett's* A Manual of Aquatic Plants. Vols. I and II. Madison: University of Wisconsin Press.

Curtis, John T. 1987. *The Vegetation of Wisconsin: An Ordination of Plant Communities.* Madison: University of Wisconsin Press.

Fernald, Merritt Lyndon, and Alfred C. Kinsey. Revised by Reed C. Rollins. 1996. *Edible Wild Plants of Eastern North America.* New York: Dover Publications.

Gleason, Henry A., and Arthur Cronquist. 1991. *Manual of Vascular Plants of North-Eastern United States and Adjacent Canada.* 2nd ed. New York: The New York Botanical Garden.

Good, R. E., D. F. Wigham, and R. L. Simpson, eds. 1978. *Freshwater Wetlands—Ecological Processes and Management Potential.* New York: Academic Press.

Holmgren, Noel H., Patricia K. Holmgren, Arthur Cronquist, and Henry A. Gleason. 2004. *Illustrated Companion to Gleason and Cronquist's Manual: Illustrations of the Vascular Plants of Northeastern United States and Adjacent Canada.* Bronx: New York Botanical Garden.

Homoya, Michael A. 1993. *Orchids of Indiana.* Bloomington: Indiana University Press.

Hotchkiss, Neil. 1964. *Pondweeds and Pondweedlike Plants of Eastern North America.* Washington, D.C.: U.S. Government Printing Office.

Hutchinson, G. Evelyn. 1957–1993. *A Treatise on Limnology.* 4 vols. New York: Wiley.

Jackson, Marion T., ed. 1997. *The Natural Heritage of Indiana.* Bloomington: Indiana University Press.

Likens, Gene E., ed. 1985. *An Ecosystem Approach to Aquatic Ecology: Mirror Lake and Its Environment.* New York: Springer-Verlag.

Likens, G. E., and F. H. Bormann. 1974. "Linkages between Terrestrial and Aquatic Ecosystems." *Bioscience* 24: 447–456.

Lindeman, Raymond Laurel. 1960. *The Trophic-Dynamic Aspect of Ecology.* Indianapolis: Bobbs-Merrill. Reprint series in the life sciences; from *Ecology* 23, no. 4 (Oct. 1942): 399–418.

Lindsey, Alton A., ed. 1976. *Natural Features of Indiana: A Symposium Held April 22–23, 1966, at Wabash College, Crawfordsville, Indiana.* Notre Dame, Indiana: American Midland Naturalist. (Reprint of 1966 edition by Indianapolis: Indiana Academy of Science.)

Lindsey, Alton A., Damian V. Schmelz, and Stanley A. Nichols. 1970. *Natural Areas in Indiana and Their Preservation: The Report of the Indiana Natural Areas Survey.* Notre Dame, Indiana: American Midland Naturalist. (Reprint of 1969 edition by Lafayette: Indiana Natural Areas Survey, Dept. of Biological Sciences, Purdue University.)

Macan, T. T. 1974. *Freshwater Ecology.* 2nd ed. New York: Wiley.

Maitland, Peter S. 1990. *Biology of Fresh Waters.* 2nd ed. New York: Chapman and Hall.

Martin, Laura C. 1984. *Wildflower Folklore.* Chester, Conn.: The Globe Pequot Press.

Mitsch, W. J., ed. 1994. *Global Wetlands: Old World and New.* Amsterdam: Elsevier.

Mitsch, W. J., and J. G. Gosselink. 2000. *Wetlands.* 3rd ed. New York: John Wiley and Sons.

Muenscher, Walter Conrad Leopold. 1972. *Aquatic Plants of the United States.* Ithaca, N.Y.: Comstock Publishing Associates, Cornell University Press.

National Research Council. 1992. *Restoration of Aquatic Ecosystems: Science, Technology, and Public Policy.* Washington, D.C.: National Academy Press. Thomas F. Nalepa and Donald W. Schloesser, eds. 1992. *Zebra Mussels: Biology, Impacts, and Control.* Boca Raton, Fla.: Lewis Publishers.

Reid, George Kell, Herbert Spencer Zim, George S. Fichter, Tom Dolan, and Sally Diana Kaicher. 2001. *Pond Life: A Guide to Common Plants and Animals of North American Ponds and Lakes.* Rev. and updated. New York: St. Martin's Press.

Sculthorpe, Cyril Duncan. 1967. *The Biology of Aquatic Vascular Plants.* New York: St. Martin's Press.

Watts, May Theilgaard. 1999. *Reading the Landscape of America*. Rochester, N.Y.: Nature Study Guild Publishers. (Reprint of rev. and exp. edition [of 1957 ed.] published 1975 by New York: Macmillan.)

Wetzel, Robert G. 1983. *Limnology*. Philadelphia: W. B. Saunders.

Torkel Korling's Wildflower Photography

Botanical illustrations and prints from nature

1958. *Wild Flowers!* Portfolio 16½ x 22 inches. 11 plates. Published and distributed by Container Corporation of America, Chicago. Out of print.

1960. *Glory by the Wayside.* Book 5 x 7½ inches. 21 plates. Published and distributed by R. R. Donnelley & Sons Company, Chicago. Out of print.

1963. *Spring Wild Flowers.* Classroom study prints 13 x 18 inches. 8 plates. Society for Visual Education, Chicago.

1963. *Wild Plants in Flower.* Portfolio 16 x 22 inches. 8 plates: Plates xlii–xlix. Second printing, 1966, for Field Museum of Natural History, Chicago, 4 plates. Out of print.

Wild Plants in Flower. Habitat series, with Diane F. Korling, editor. Books 4½ x 6⅞ inches:

Books

1972. *The Prairie—Swell and Swale.* Text by Robert F. Betz. Out of print.

1973. *The Boreal Forest and Borders.* Text by Edward G. Voss. Out of print.

1974. *Deciduous Forest.* Text by Robert O. Petty. Revised edition, 1977, as *Eastern Deciduous Forest.* Out of print.

Index to Plants Pictured

Nomenclature according to Gleason and Cronquist, 1991; family names updated.

Acorus calamus	77
Alisma subcordatum	69
Angelica atropurpurea	17
Asclepias incarnata	47
Bidens cernua	85
Bidens laevis	57
Calla palustris	75
Caltha palustris	cover
Carex lacustris	25
Cephalanthus occidentalis	89
Cirsium muticum	49
Cypripedium acaule	title page frontis
Eupatorium perfoliatum	27
Eupatorium purpureum	31
Habenaria lacera	71
Hibiscus moscheutos	9
Hydrocotyle umbellata	81
Iris virginica	63
Lemna minor	41
Lobelia cardinalis	87
Lysimachia terrestris	59
Lysimachia thyrsiflora	55
Mentha arvensis	21
Menyanthes trifoliata	73
Nelumbo lutea	11

Nuphar advena	41
Nuphar variegata	79
Nymphaea odorata	39
Nymphoides cordata	53
Orontium aquaticum	37
Pedicularis lanceolata	65
Peltandra virginica	45
Polygonum amphibium	33
Pontederia cordata	35
Potamogeton natans	5
Potentilla palustris	29
Ptilimnium capillaceum	15
Ranunculus flabellaris	43
Ranunculus gmelinii	25
Ranunculus sceleratus	19
Rorippa nasturium-aquaticum	67
Sagittaria latifolia	83
Saururus cernuus	23
Scirpus pungens	15
Sparganium eurycarpum	51
Symplocarpus foetidus	13
Typha angustifolia	7
Utricularia cornuta	61
Angelica, Purplestem	17
Arrow-arum	45
Arrowhead	83
Beggar-tick	57
Bladderwort	61
Boneset	27
Buckbean	73
Bur-marigold, Nodding	85
Bur-reed	51
Buttonbush	89
Cardinal-flower	87
Cat-tail, Narrow-leaved	7

Chair-maker's rush	15
Cinquefoil, Marsh	29
Crowfoot, Common Cursed	19
Crowfoot, Small Yellow Water	25
Crowfoot, Yellow Water	43
Duckweed	41
Floating-heart	53
Golden-club	37
Iris, Southern-blue	63
Joe-Pye weed	31
Lizard's-tail	23
Lotus Lily	11
Lousewort, Swamp	65
Marsh marigold	cover
Milkweed, Swamp	47
Mint, Field	21
Moccasin Flower	title page frontis
Mock Bishop's-weed	15
Orchid, Ragged Fringed	71
Pickerel-weed	35
Pond-lily, Yellow	41
Pondweed, Floating-leaved	5
Rose-mallow	9
Sedge	25
Skunk-cabbage	13
Smartweed, Water	33
Spatterdock, Variegated	79
Swamp-candles	59
Swamp-loosestrife	55
Sweet-flag	77
Thistle, Swamp	49
Water-arum	75
Watercress	67
Water-lily, Fragrant	39
Water-pennywort	81
Water-plantain	69

BOOK AND JACKET DESIGNER
Sharon L. Sklar

COPY EDITOR
Miki Bird

COMPOSITOR
Sharon L. Sklar

TYPEFACE
New Caledonia

BOOK AND JACKET PRINTER
Four Colour Imports